Ladders

WELCOME TO
KENYA
AROUND THE WORLD

Welcome to

KENYA !

by Stephanie Herbek

In the African country of Kenya, most days are hot, dry, and sunny. Cheetahs, elephants, giraffes, and many other animals roam freely on **savannas**, or lands covered with grasses and other plants. They seek shade under wide, leafy trees that shelter them from the scorching afternoon sun.

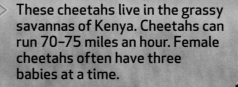

These cheetahs live in the grassy savannas of Kenya. Cheetahs can run 70–75 miles an hour. Female cheetahs often have three babies at a time.

Animals aren't the only living things in Kenya. More than 40 million people live there, too. Most of them live in **villages**. A village is a community that is smaller than a city and is usually located in the country. Many people who live in villages work on farms. They spend long, hot hours planting crops in their fields.

Other Kenyans live in the city. Just like in the United States, they take a bus or drive through busy streets to get to their jobs. They work in offices, factories, and schools. Let's find out more about the people and communities of Kenya.

Straw Huts and Skyscrapers

Some Kenyans live in villages mostly made up of **tribes**, or groups of people that share the same language, way of life, and beliefs. Most villagers' homes are cozy huts made of sticks and mud. A fire pit in the center of each hut makes cooking food easy. Villagers get water by pulling it up from deep underground wells.

Villagers keep very busy tending to their farms, and they grow much of the food they eat. One type of food they grow in their fields is cassava, a vegetable that is a little like a potato. Villagers also care for their cows and goats. These animals give villagers milk to drink and to sell in markets.

Kenyan huts are designed well. Their straw roofs shelter people from the hot sun. Huts also keep villagers dry when it rains.

> People sell their crops and farm animals at markets. This colorful market is in the center of a Kenyan village.

Other Kenyans live in cities such as Nairobi (nih-ROH-bee), the capital city of Kenya. Nairobi is the largest city in the country. More than three million people live there. This city has libraries, skyscrapers, and restaurants, just like big cities in other parts of the world. Most people in Nairobi live in apartment buildings or houses made of flat sheets of metal. They zoom through the busy streets in minivans called *matatos*, or ride motorcycles and bikes.

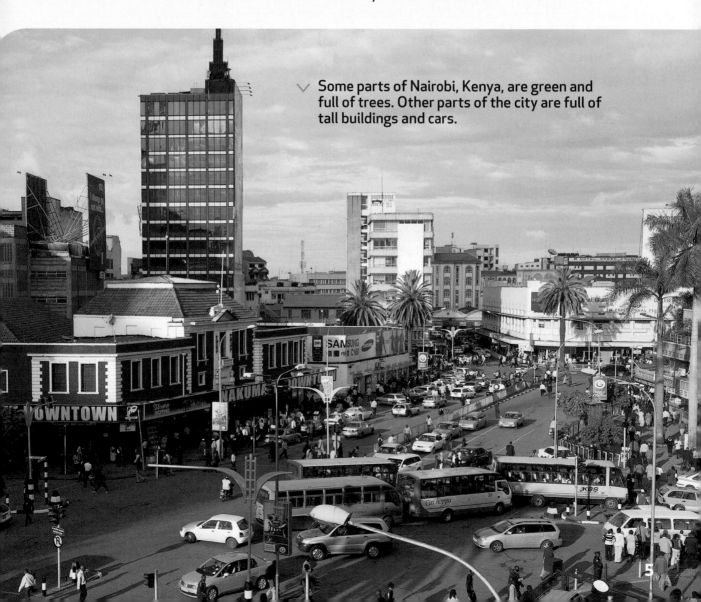

> Some parts of Nairobi, Kenya, are green and full of trees. Other parts of the city are full of tall buildings and cars.

Time for School, Time for Fun

Most children who live in Kenyan villages walk to school every morning. They start the day with a song and then learn how to speak Swahili (swuh-HEE-lee). This is the language that people speak in Kenya and in many other African countries. The students study outside together at tables under trees. Sometimes they can hear the sounds of birds chirping during their math and spelling lessons. It must be exciting to share a classroom with wild animals!

Not all children go to school in their village. Some of them attend schools far away from home. Other children help with farmwork instead of going to school.

Schools in the cities of Kenya are like many in the United States. Some students wear uniforms to school, and others wear regular clothes. The children work at tables in large classrooms. At some city schools, students use computers. Just like you, students may walk or take the bus to and from school.

The weather in Kenya is sunny and warm—perfect for playing outside. What sports do Kenyan children play after school? They love to play soccer, basketball, and volleyball when school and chores are done.

tafadhali (TAH-fah-DAH-lee) means "please"

asante (ah-SAHN-tay) means "thank you"

Habari? (hah-BAR-ee) means "How are you?"

kwaheri (kwah-HAIR-ee) means "good-bye"

⌄ Some classes in Kenya are held outdoors. Imagine seeing an elephant walk by while you are at school!

Check In How is school in Kenya different from what school is like where you live? How is it similar?

GENRE Folk Tale

Read to find out whether strength or cleverness is more important.

Elephant and Hare

a Traditional Kenyan Folk Tale

retold by Jenny Loomis   *illustrated by Gerald Guerlais*

*A folk tale is a story that teaches **values**, or beliefs about what is important and how people should behave. This folk tale is based on a story from Kenya. The elephant in the tale represents strength. The **hare**, an animal similar to a rabbit but larger, represents **cleverness**, or intelligence. Some folk tales explain why animals look the way they do. This folk tale explains why hares have short tails.*

As day was fading to night, Hare stood at the edge of a river, looking down at the water. She needed to get home before Fox came out for his nightly hunt. She would have to shorten her journey by crossing the river, but she didn't feel strong enough to swim through the deep water.

Just then, Elephant came thundering across the field. He ran up to Hare and began laughing. "I see you can't cross the river. That's too bad, because swimming is so easy for me!"

"Elephant, please wait," said Hare. "Could I ride on your back as you swim across the river? I'm afraid Fox will find me before I can get home safely to my children and give them this big pot of honey." Hare opened her basket and showed Elephant a golden pot of honey.

Elephant brightened when he heard the word "honey" because this was his favorite sweet treat. He could eat honey all day, every day.

"I will carry you across the river if you give me your honey pot," Elephant said.

"But this honey is a gift for my children," said Hare sadly.

"Fine. Then I am leaving. Do say 'hello' to Fox for me," said Elephant rudely.

Hare knew she had to get herself and her honey home before dark, so she quickly came up with a clever plan. "Okay, you can have the honey," agreed Hare.

"That's a very smart decision, Hare. Hop on so we can get going!" Elephant ordered triumphantly.

Elephant carried Hare across the river. When they reached the other side, he lifted his trunk up over his head, waiting for the honey pot. Instead, Hare placed an empty drinking cup into Elephant's waiting trunk. Then she jumped off his back and dashed toward her home. Elephant was too busy admiring his powerful trunk to notice that Hare had fooled him.

When he realized he had been tricked, Elephant angrily threw the empty cup on the ground and ran to catch up to Hare. His powerful legs drew him closer and closer. Hare dashed and dodged and dove into a hole, but Elephant reached out and caught her by her long tail. To both of their surprise, Hare's long, glorious tail snapped off, leaving her with nothing but a puff.

Frustrated and surprised, Elephant threw the tail aside and stuck his long trunk down the hole to try to reach Hare, but it quickly became tangled in a tree root. While he struggled and fussed, Hare managed to escape. She ran to a large group of hares standing nearby.

Hare knew she couldn't hide from Elephant for very long. She needed to blend in with the other hares, but they all had long tails. Hare quickly thought of a clever way to blend in. She hid her basket in some bushes, joined the group of hares, and yelled, "Hurry! You must remove your long tails! Elephant is coming and he's very angry. He's looking for hares with long tails!"

The frightened hares had just finished removing their long tails when Elephant arrived. He was huffing and puffing from the chase and he was very angry. He didn't like being tricked by a little hare and he wanted that honey now more than ever. "Hares!" he screamed. "I'm looking for the hare with the short tail! Those of you with long tails must step to one side."

The group of little hares slowly and carefully walked toward Elephant. With much relief, they turned around and revealed their new, short tails.

"Oh, peanuts. That hare has tricked me again!" trumpeted Elephant. Having had enough of clever hares for one day, he stomped away.

Hare fetched her basket and ran as fast as she could toward her home. When she arrived, she fed her hungry children the honey and showed them her new, short tail. They all admired it and shortened their own tails to match their mother's. Hare also told them about the elephant. "Children, you may not be as big and strong as other animals," Hare remarked, "but you are all very smart. When you find yourself in trouble, try to think of a solution. Problems don't usually get solved simply by being big or strong."

The children were thankful to have such a smart mother. They each gave her a big sticky hug and happily ate the rest of the delicious honey.

Check In How does Hare trick Elephant?

If you are lucky enough to visit Kenya's savanna, you may catch a glimpse of a tall man dressed in bright red clothing walking through the grass. He's most likely a Maasai (muh-SY) man, walking with a large herd of cattle, or cows. The Maasai people live in Kenya. They are **nomads**, which means they move from place to place very often. They don't move just for fun. They move to find places with plenty of fresh grass for their cattle to eat.

< Maasai men have to walk many miles each day. They must move their cattle to grassy areas.

The
Mighty

The Maasai treat their cattle very well. Maasai men are usually in charge of the herds, and they often give their cows names. Sometimes they even sing to them! The Maasai think of their cattle as family members. The cattle are shown this level of respect, or honor, because they give the Maasai what they need to live comfortable, healthful lives. Herds of cattle provide the Maasai with milk, meat, and leather. They are very useful animals.

by Sean O'Shea

Milk, Meat, and Medicine

Cattle provide important food for the Maasai. But the Maasai don't eat the cow's meat very often—only during special celebrations. It is the cows' milk that is very important to the Maasai because it makes up most of their diet. In fact, a cup of milk is a common meal for the Maasai. They also use milk to make many other foods.

In the morning, the Maasai might drink milk or spiced milky tea called *chai* (CHY), or eat a porridge made from corn flour, milk, water, and sugar. They call this porridge *ugi*. The Maasai also eat yogurt made from their cows' milk.

Sometimes the Maasai nibble on tree bark between meals. If that seems strange, consider this: if you've eaten anything with cinnamon in it, you've eaten tree bark, too! The Maasai use tree bark to flavor soup, just like we might use cinnamon to flavor oatmeal. They also use tree bark as medicine for an upset stomach.

Owning cattle is a lot of work. Maasai men spend their days herding the animals. Maasai women milk the cattle twice a day.

How to Make Kenyan Chai Tea

Chai tea is a very popular drink in Kenya. It is tea mixed with milk, sugar, and spices. Many children drink chai in the morning before going to school.

1. Pour 2 cups of water and 2 cups of milk into a saucepan.

2. Add 1½ teaspoons of black tea leaves (or more, if you like strong tea) to the water and milk in the saucepan.

3. Add some spices such as cinnamon, cardamom, and ginger to the saucepan.

4. With an adult's help, bring the mixture to a boil.

5. Turn the heat down and mix the tea with a spoon until it tastes strong enough.

6. Add a little sugar to sweeten the tea, and stir.

7. Remove the tea leaves from the saucepan.

8. Pour the spiced tea into a mug and enjoy!

19

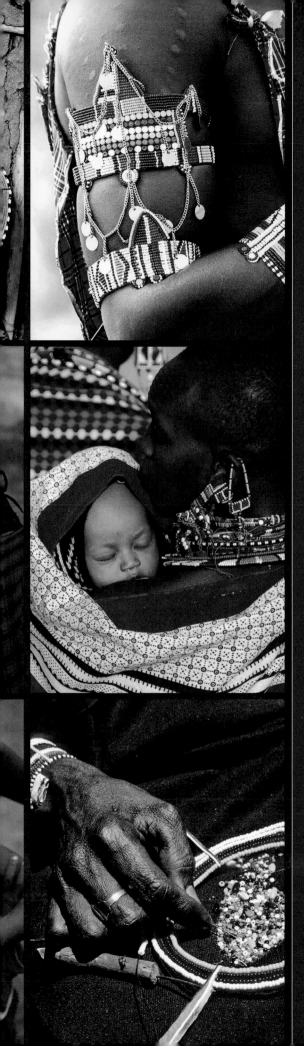

The Power of Red

The Maasai wear clothing that keeps them cool and comfortable in Kenya's sunny, warm weather. Their clothing and shoes are often made from animal skins. But the Maasai have also started to wear cotton because it keeps them cooler. Since their villages are far away from markets, they even make clothes out of things they find around their homes and while traveling. For example, some Maasai make sandals out of old car tires! Most of all, the Maasai enjoy wearing brightly colored clothing. Red is an important color to the Maasai because it **symbolizes**, or stands for, power.

The Maasai make beautifully decorated jewelry in many different colors. For them, glass and clay beads are common **ornaments**, or things that add beauty. They also string together metal, seeds, ivory, bone, horns, shells, leather, and feathers. They wear this jewelry in the form of earrings, necklaces, and bracelets. Sometimes young men and women wear special jewelry to attract each other.

Jumping for Joy

Jumping is part of a Maasai dance called *adumu*. In this dance, young Maasai **warriors** take turns jumping in the middle of a circle. A Maasai warrior is a young man who learns how to hunt and how to protect his family. Each warrior makes sure that his heels never touch the ground as he sings and jumps higher and higher. Who will win this jumping contest? The man who jumps the highest, of course! The Maasai believe that the highest adumu jumper is the strongest warrior.

Maasai males become warriors when they are in their teens. After about ten years of being a warrior, they are ready to become adults. They dance adumu to celebrate the end of their warrior years and the beginning of adulthood. Once they are adults, the men can get married, have children, and raise cattle. Then new young Maasai men become warriors and adumu dancers.

Two Maasai warriors show their strength by jumping high into the air.

Check In Why are cattle important to the Maasai?

Discuss

1. Tell about some of the ways you think the three selections in this book are linked.

2. How is living in a village in Kenya different from living in a city?

3. What are some important things you have learned about the Maasai way of life?

4. In the folk tale, Hare is clever and Elephant is strong. Do you think cleverness or strength is more important? Why?

5. What do you still wonder about Kenya and the people who live there?